Learning LOL

Welcome to my class about fun facts about animals! My name is Professor Charlie, and I am so excited to show you all the fun things my assistant and I have been learning. My assistant is my mom, and she is super helpful! She reads all of the research we do together out loud, takes me for walks when it is time for a break, finds yummy treats for the both of us to share, and also does all the typing since she has fingers and thumbs, and I only have paws, and the most important thing of all, she gives the best belly rubs. My job is to give her fun ideas to look up, to keep her warm with cuddles, and to try not to bark at the mailman. I make no promises about the last one. We make a really great team!

Late one afternoon, my assistant and I needed a break from our work day. We love to go for walks in the park, so we decided to go on one. It was warm and sunny, so it was perfect for a walk. As we entered the park, we saw a small brown animal with a white tummy and a long, brown and, white, fluffy tail that I had never seen before. I asked my assistant if she knew what it was, and she told me it was a squirrel. She also told me this would be a wonderful time to make a new friend, and I agreed. We walked up to the little squirrel and introduced ourselves. She told us her name was Sally. With the biggest grin and my tail wagging as fast as it could, I told her I was a dog, and this was my human. Sally gave a little smile and said she was a squirrel. I told her she was the first squirrel I had ever met and talked to. I asked her if she had ever talked to a dog before, and she said no. They normally bark and chase her. This made me a little sad. I asked her if my assistant and I could stay and talk for a little while to get to know each other, and maybe we could play together. She excitedly said yes, so we sat in the shade of a tree, asking each other all the questions we could think of and sharing our snack of orange slices and watermelon pieces. When we were done with our snack I knew about squirrels, like what they like to eat and where they lived, and Sally knew all about dogs. After the yummy snack, I was ready to play before returning home, so I asked Sally if she would like to run around and play. She instantly jumped up with a smile and was ready to run. We played tag all around the park, and Sally made sure she didn't run up any trees because that would not be fair since I couldn't climb trees. Wow, who knew squirrels were so fast? After about 20 minutes, my assistant told me it was time to go. We were all sad that the fun had to end, but we told Sally that we would come back to the park very soon! She thanked us for sharing our snack and playing tag with her. She told me that this was the first time she had ever been able to chase a dog, and this was also the first time she had had fun having a dog chase her. We all had a really big laugh, said our goodbyes, and started our walk home.

After we returned home, my assistant and I were relaxing on the cozy sofa, eating our favorite snack (peanut butter & apples), and I was thinking about our walk. I asked her what other kinds of animals were out there. My mom, sorry, I meant my assistant, said there were so many different kinds of animals. She said that some animals can swim in the deep ocean or fly over the tallest mountain. I was so happy to hear this that my tail began to wag really hard. I thought it was going to fly away. This was so exciting! I quickly jumped up from the sofa, gently got my assistant's laptop for her, and placed it on her lap. I then put my head on her lap, looked up at her, gave her the biggest puppy dog eyes, and asked if we could look up some more animals. Of course, she said yes because my puppy eyes always worked, and my mom loves to learn! We had so much fun looking up all of these different animals. Who knew that animals could look so different from each other but still have some things in common? It is just amazing! Then I had an idea!

I told my assistant we had such a great time learning about these different animals that we needed to share this information with you, my new pup pal! So, that is what we did. My assistant and I sat down, found all the best fun facts about these animals, and wrote this book for you! Please don't worry if you don't understand something that I wrote because I made sure everything was super easy to look up if you didn't understand. Looking up things you don't know is a wonderful way for you to learn how to be a researcher like me! But please ask an adult if it is ok to use the computer before you begin your research. Manners and safety first! I hope you enjoy our book, our new pup pal. We will see you for your next lesson!

Tara & Charlie Morrish

Photos by
Scarlet Morrish

Professor Charlie

Smokey

Learninglol.com

![Learning LOL - Where learning language online is fun!]

Learning About the Creatures Around Us!

We want to thank you, from the bottom of our paws to the tips of our ears, for buying our book! We hope you enjoyed reading it as much as we enjoyed writing and researching it. We are also excited to share that you can join us on our website soon. Here, you can view your favorite topics with videos, maps, pictures, interactive worksheets, and flashcards. To make entering the classroom easier, scan the QR code, but remember to ask your grown-up before going online. See you there!

Have fun learning online!   *Have fun learning with more books!*

Learning About the Creatures Around Us!

Table of Contents

Learning About the Creatures Around Us!

7 continents map with 5 oceans

Army Ants

★**Animal class**: **Insects** (Have a segmented body (3 main body parts: the head, the thorax, and the abdomen), are cold-blooded, have an exoskeleton (an outer skeleton around the whole body to help protect them), jointed legs, six legs, antennas, wings (some insect will have 1-2 pairs of wings or no wings at all), most babies come from eggs, but some are live births, and their sizes range from the **Dicopomorpha echmepterygis (a type of wasp, also called a Fairyfly)** at 0.005 in (.139 mm) to the **Phoebaeticus chani (a type of Stick insect)** at 2 ft (62.4 cm) long. **(Examples: Beetles, butterflies, Praying mantis, and ladybugs) There are around 925 thousand different species)**

★**Diet**: **Carnivores (They only eat meat)**- feed on other ants and insects and on some smaller animals like frogs, snakes, and lizards

★**Lifespan:** The queen can live up to 20 years, worker ants about one year

★**Predators:** Birds, beetles, and wasps

★**Size**: Worker ants (0.25 in or 0.635 cm), Soldier ants (0.5 in or 1.27 cm), Drone ants (0.60 in or 1.5 cm), Queen is the largest (2 in or 5 cm)

★**Species**: There are over 200 ant species

★**Status**: Not Endangered

Learning About the Creatures Around Us!

★**Weight**: About 0.00004 -0.0002 oz (1-5 mg)

★**Where do they live?**: They can be found in every continent but Antarctica

★They make a temporary nest out of their bodies called "bivouacs" and can hold 200,000 ants or more. These nests can be found inside or hanging from trees or large structures it can hang from. Inside the nest are the queen and the larvae (baby ants & eggs). The ants move their nest about every 25 days to make room for new ants.

★About every three years, the colony will split into two groups. They do this because the colony gets too big.

★These ants are not generally dangerous but will bite and sting.

★Army ants work collectively to build bridges out of their bodies, and they can be many feet (meters) long. This body bridge helps them get from one place to another when there is an open space in between.

★Once in a while, a smaller group of army ants will separate from the leading group of ants, and when this happens, they will start to follow each other in a circle. When the ants start to do this, it is called a "death spiral" because they will never stop following one another and die from exhaustion (from being too tired).

Learning About the Creatures Around Us!

Axolotl

★**Animal class**: **Amphibians** (Have vertebrae (backbone or spine), are cold-blooded (their bodies cannot hold heat and must warm themselves by their surroundings like the sun), and can live on land and in the water, they lay their eggs in the water after the eggs hatch they go through metamorphosis (their bodies change) and start as a tadpole with gills, and will then change into their adult form and grow 4 legs and lungs, their skin does not have fur or feathers and helps them take in oxygen, and their sizes from the **Paedophryne amauensis (a type of frog)** at 0.27 in (0.7 mm) to the **Chinese giant salamander** at 6ft (2 m)) **(Examples: Frog, toads, salamanders, and newts. There are over 8,000 different species)**

★**Diet**: **Carnivore (They only eat meat)**: Worms, insects, shrimp, and tadpoles

★**Lifespan**: 10-15 years

★**Predators**: Large fish and birds

★**Size**: Up to 12 in (30 cm) long

★**Species**: There are only 1 species, but there are about 15 different color types

★**Speed:** About 10 mph (16 kph)

Learning About the Creatures Around Us!

★**<u>Status</u>**: Critically Endangered, about 1,000 left in the wild

★**<u>Weight</u>**: About 2 to 8 oz (60-227 g)

★**<u>Where do they live?</u>**: They live in Lake Xochimilco and its canals in Mexico, near the edge of Mexico City.

★They are aquatic (live in water) salamanders.

★They are neoteny, meaning they look almost identical in their baby and adult forms.

★They have feathery external gills (antennae) on their heads, which is how they breathe.

★They can completely regenerate an entire limb (arm, leg, or tail) when lost. They can even regrow parts of their heart, lungs, brain, and other organs in a few weeks.

★Every so often, the axolotl swims to the water's surface and breathes air. Along with gills, they also have fully working lungs.

★Axolotls also do not have eyelids, so they can't blink and sleep with their eyes open.

Learning About the Creatures Around Us!

Aye-Aye

★**Animal class**: **Mammals -** (They are warm-blooded (the body temperature stays about the same temperature without help from the sun), breathe air with lungs, have a 4 chamber heart, have 3 bones in their inner ears, have vertebrae (a backbone or spine), have hair or fur (even whales and dolphins have some hair near their mouths), almost all species have a live birth, but 2 species lay eggs (the platypus and the echidna), all females produce (their bodies make) milk for their young, most have 4 legs or for humans, 2 arms and 2 legs, sizes range from the **Bumblebee bat** at 1 in (3 cm) to the **Blue whale** at 100 ft (30 m)) **(Examples: Whales, people, dogs, and elephants. There are about 6,500 different species.)**

★**Diet**: **Omnivore (They eat plants and meat)**- Insects and fruit

★**Lifespan**: 20-years

★**Predators**: Fossa 23 and large birds

★**Size**: 16 in (40 cm) long & their bushy tail 22-24 in (55-60 cm) long

★**Species**: There are only 1 species of long-fingered lemur, but there are around 100 different species of lemurs

★**Speed:** About 20 mph (32 kph)

Learning About the Creatures Around Us!

★**Status**: Endangered (not many left) between 1,000-10,000

★**Weight**: 4 lbs. (1.81 kg)

★**Where do they live?**: They are native to Madagascar

★They have a special thin middle finger that they use to find prey hiding inside trees.

★They use echolocation (sound bouncing off an object) to help find their prey hiding inside the trees (the only primate to use it). They will tap on the tree's branches to find their prey. They will dig a hole into the tree's bark with their sharp claws and dig it out with their long finger.

★They are nocturnal (awake at night) and are the largest primate to do so.

★They spend most of their time in trees and make ball-like nests toward the tops of these trees.

★These animals are mostly solitary (live by themselves) but hunt in pairs.

Learning About the Creatures Around Us!

Barbados Threadsnake

★**Animal class**: **Reptiles**- (Their bodies are covered in bony plates or scales, they breathe air with lungs, are cold-blooded (their bodies cannot hold heat and must warm themselves by their surroundings like the sun), have vertebrae (spine or backbone), most have 4 legs, they lay eggs (Some species like the Viper (snake) will keep their eggs in their bodies until the egg hatches. Then the baby is born. A few rare species have a live birth like the Three-toed skink), and their sizes range from the **Brookesia nana (a chameleon)** at .55 in (1.4 cm) to the **Saltwater crocodile** at 20 ft (6 m)) **(Example: Lizards, turtles, snakes, and alligators. There are about 9,000 different species.)**

★**Diet**: **Carnivore (They only eat meat)**- Termites and insect larvae (babies or eggs)

★**Lifespan**: Unknown

★**Predators:** Birds and other bigger animals

★**Size**: About 4.1 in (10 cm) long

★**Species**: There are about 15 species of threadsnakes

★**Status:** Critically Endangered

★**Weight**: About 0.02 oz (0.6 g)

Learning About the Creatures Around Us!

★**Where do they live?**: They live in the forest in the Caribbean on the island of Barbados.

★They are the smallest known snake species.

★They are completely harmless, not poisonous.

★They live in the forest and spend most of their time burrowing underground, searching for food.

★Females only lay one egg at a time, and it is shaped like a grain of rice. Most snakes can lay 3-100 eggs at a time.

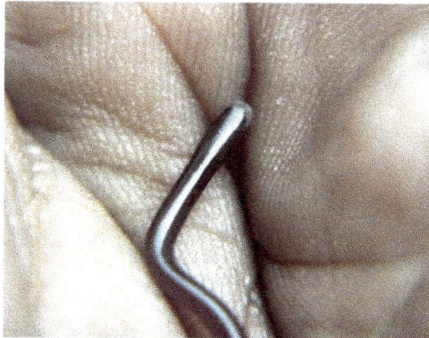

Learning About the Creatures Around Us!

Bee Hummingbird

★<u>**Animal class**</u>: **Birds** (Have feathers, a beak (no teeth), two legs, and two wings (some species cannot fly), have vertebrae (spine or backbone), are warm-blooded (the body temperature stays about the same temperature), lay eggs, might be related to dinosaurs, have a four-chamber heart (4 parts), most have excellent eyesight, and they range in size from the <u>**Bee hummingbird**</u> at 2.2 in (5.5 cm) to the <u>**Ostrich**</u> at 9 ft (3 m) tall) **(Examples: Penguins, parrots, owls, and hawks) There are around 11,000 different species)**

★<u>**Diet**</u>: **Omnivore (They eat plants and meat)**- Nectar, small insects, and spiders

★<u>**Lifespan**</u>: About seven years

★<u>**Predators**</u>: Hawks, falcons, fish, frogs, and spiders

★<u>**Size**</u>: Females 2.4 in (6 cm) tall, Males 2.2 in (5.5 cm) tall

★<u>**Species**</u>: There are about 325 species of hummingbirds

★<u>**Speed:**</u> About 25-30 mph (40-48 kph)

★<u>**Status**</u>: Near Threatened

★<u>**Weight**</u>: Females 0.09 oz (2.6 g) & Males 0.07 oz (1.95 g)

Learning About the Creatures Around Us!

★**Where do they live?**: They live in Cuba, in the rainforest, along the coast, and in wooded areas.

★They are the world's smallest birds.

★Their tiny wings beat up to 70 times per second, but during mating season, they can beat up to 200 times per second.

★They can fly up to 20 hours without stopping.

★Their hearts beat up to 1,200 beats per minute.

★Their eggs are also the smallest in the world and the size of a coffee bean.

★During mating season, the male's feathers on its chin, chest, and head will turn a pinkish color to help attract a female.

★They are the only birds able to fly backward, straight up, and upside down.

Learning About the Creatures Around Us!

Beluga Whale

★**Animal class**: **Mammals**- (They are warm-blooded (the body temperature stays about the same temperature without help from the sun), breathe air with lungs, have a 4 chamber heart, have 3 bones in their inner ears, have vertebrae (a backbone or spine), have hair or fur (even whales and dolphins have some hair near their mouths), almost all species have a live birth, but 2 species lay eggs (the platypus and the echidna), all females produce (their bodies make) milk for their young, most have 4 legs or for humans, 2 arms and 2 legs, sizes range from the **Bumblebee bat** at 1 in (3 cm) to the **Blue whale** at 100 ft (30 m)) **(Examples: Whales, people, dogs, and elephants. There are about 6,500 different species.)**

★**Diet**: **Carnivore (They only eat meat)**- Salmon and herring, as well as shrimp, crabs, and mollusks

★**Lifespan**: 35–50 years

★**Predators**: Polar bears and killer whales (orcas)

★**Size**: 8.5-22 ft (259- 670 cm) long

★**Species**: There are about 90 different species of whales, but the Beluga whale's closest relative is the narwhal.

★**Speed:** About 17 mph (27 kmh)

Learning About the Creatures Around Us!

★<u>**Status**</u>: Endangered

★<u>**Weight**</u>: 1,500-3,500 lbs. (up to 680-1,600 kg)

★<u>**Where do they live?**</u>: They live in the Arctic Ocean.

★They are brilliant and social animals. They live in groups called "pods."

★They are called "Sea Canaries," belugas are one of the most vocal of all whales.

★The rounded structure on their forehead is called a "melon." Belugas wiggle their melons like a microphone to focus sounds in specific directions.

★They can dive underwater for up to 25 minutes.

★They hunt in groups and will herd their prey to shallower water. Hunting in groups makes it easier for the whales to eat. They swallow it whole when they catch their prey and don't chew their food.

★Belugas can eat up to 60 lbs. (27 kg) daily.

★They also have the special ability to turn their necks up and down and left and right, which is helpful for hunting. Other whales and dolphins cannot do this.

Learning About the Creatures Around Us!

Black Mamba

★**Animal class**: **Reptiles**- (Their bodies are covered in bony plates or scales, they breathe air with lungs, are cold-blooded (their bodies cannot hold heat and must warm themselves by their surroundings like the sun), have vertebrae (spine or backbone), most have 4 legs, they lay eggs (Some species like the Viper (snake) will keep their eggs in their bodies until the egg hatches. Then the baby is born. A few rare species have a live birth like the Three-toed skink), and their sizes range from the **Brookesia nana (a chameleon)** at .55 in (1.4 cm) to the **Saltwater crocodile** at 20 ft (6 m)) **(Example: Lizards, turtles, snakes, and alligators. There are about 9,000 different species.)**

★**Diet**: **Carnivore (They only eat meat)**: Birds, mice, other types of snakes, bats, bush babies, mongooses, and other small mammals

★**Lifespan**: About 11 years

★**Predators**: Mongooses, foxes, giant birds, and jackals

★**Size**: About 8-14 ft (2-4 m) long

★**Species**: There are four different species of Black mamba, but there are over 3,000 different species of snakes.

★**Speed**: About 14 mph (23 kph)

★**Status**: Least Concern

★**Weight**: About 4 lbs. (2 kg)

★**Where do they live?**: They live in the northern part of southern Africa, in the rocky hills, wooded lands, and the savannas

★It is Africa's deadliest snake.

★The inside of their mouth is black, which is supposed to help scare off their predators. Their mouth is also where they get their names. Their bodies are tan (light brown), olive (light green), and darker brown.

★They are highly venomous and shy, but when threatened, they are aggressive and can kill a person with two drops of venom, but there is a cure if given in about 20 minutes.

★When these snakes are born, they already have venom in their fangs.

★These snakes can swim.

★At night, they burrow in the ground, and during the day, they can be found in trees lying in the sun.

Learning About the Creatures Around Us!

Blobfish

★<u>**Animal class**</u>: **Fish** (Have vertebrae (a backbone or spine), have gills instead of lungs, are cold-blooded (their bodies cannot hold heat and must warm themselves by their surroundings like the sun), have fins to help them get around, most have scales, most do not have eyelids, have a swim bladder (helps them control how deep they go in the water), they have a 2 chamber heart, their ears are inside their bodies, they lay eggs that will, but some females will carry their fertilized eggs and give live birth (only a few species do this), and their sizes range from a male **<u>Photocorynus spiniceps (a type of anglerfish)</u>** 0.2 in (6.1 mm) to the **<u>Whale shark</u>** at 42 ft (13 m)) **(Examples: Goldfish, sharks, salmon, and Sword Fish. There are over 30,000 different species)**

★<u>**Diet**</u>: **Omnivore (They eat plants and meat)**: Plants, crabs, snails, oysters, sea urchins, and pieces of dead animals that make their way down to the ocean floor

★<u>**Lifespan**</u>: About 130 years

★<u>**Predators**</u>: Only humans because of pollution, warming waters, and some fishing

★<u>**Size**</u>: About 1 ft (30 cm) long

★<u>**Species**</u>: There are about 9 different species of blobfish, but there are around 30,000 different species of fish

Learning About the Creatures Around Us!

★<u>**Speed**</u>: About 5 mph (8 kph)

★<u>**Status**</u>: Scientists are unsure how many are left since they live so deep in the ocean.

★<u>**Weight**</u>: About 20 lbs. (10 kg)

★<u>**Where do they live?**</u>: They live in the deep oceans of the Indian and Pacific Oceans

★They could be found 1,100-9,300 ft (335-2,800 m) under the ocean's surface because they do not have a swim bladder. This air-filled sac acts as a floating device for the fish, which helps keep them closer to the surface.

★They don't need hard, thick bones since they like to hang out at the bottom of the ocean floor. They do have fragile, soft bones but very few muscles. So this is why when they are out of the water, they look blob-like with funny-looking faces because they have no real bones to support their shape.

★They do not have teeth and are not active hunters. They usually lie down and wait until something floats by their mouth and then gobble it up.

Learning About the Creatures Around Us!

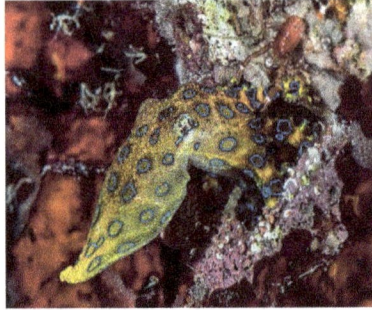

Blue-ring Octopus

★<u>**Animal class**</u>: **Mollusks** (Are invertebrates (with no backbone or spine), have an exoskeleton (an outer shell to help protect their soft bodies, and have a sharp tongue called a "radula" that helps them take food off of hard surfaces, they breathe with tiny gills called ctenidia, they lay eggs, some have a "foot" (the underside of a snail) to help them move, and their sizes range from the <u>**Acmella nana (a type of snail)**</u> at 0.02 in (0.6 mm) to the <u>**Colossal Squid**</u> at 45 ft (14 m))**(Examples: Octopus, squid, snails, and clams. There are over 80,000 different species)**

★<u>**Diet**</u>: **Carnivore (They only eat meat)**- Shrimp, small crabs, and fish

★<u>**Lifespan**</u>: About 2 years

★<u>**Predators**</u>: Birds, seals, moray eels, and whales

★<u>**Size**</u>: About 8 in (20 cm)

★<u>**Species**</u>: There are 10 different species of Blue-ring octopuses, but there are around 300 different species of octopuses.

★<u>**Speed**</u>: About 24 mph (38 kph)

Learning About the Creatures Around Us!

★<u>**Status**</u>: Not Threatened

★<u>**Weight**</u>: About 1.9 oz (54 g)

★<u>**Where do they live?**</u>: They live in the Indian and the Pacific Oceans, from Japan to Australia

★They live in shallow water in coral reefs and seagrass, under rocks and shells, and in tide pools.

★They have eight arms, nine brains, a beak, and three hearts.

★They also have light blue and sometimes brownish colored rings on their bodies that will light up and flash bright electric blue when they are threatened.

★When they attack their prey, they bite them and inject them with venomous saliva that will paralyze the prey.

★It is one of the most poisonous animals in the ocean, and one octopus could kill about 25 men within minutes, and there is no cure.

★When these octopuses are young, they will still have an ink sac and can use it. As they get older, the sac gets smaller and smaller, and the octopus will lose the ability to use their ink.

Learning About the Creatures Around Us!

Capybara

★**Animal class**: **Mammals** - (They are warm-blooded (the body temperature stays about the same temperature without help from the sun), breathe air with lungs, have a four-chamber heart, have three bones in their inner ears, have vertebrae (a backbone or spine), have hair or fur (even whales and dolphins have some hair near their mouths), almost all species have a live birth, but two species lay eggs (the platypus and the echidna), all females produce (their bodies make) milk for their young, most have four legs or for humans, two arms and two legs, sizes range from the **Bumblebee bat** at 1 in (3 cm) to the **Blue whale** at 100 ft (30 m)) **(Examples: Whales, people, dogs, and elephants. There are about 6,500 different species.)**

★**Diet**: **Herbivore (They only eat plants)**- They eat 6-8 lbs. (3-4 kg) of grass a day, sugar cane, and tree bark. They also eat their poop in the morning (this helps them digest their food better).

★**Lifespan**: Up to 7 years

★**Predators:** Snakes, jaguars, eagles, and piranha

★**Size**: 4.6 ft (140 cm) tall and up to 2 ft (60 cm) high at shoulders

★**Species**: There are two different species

★**Speed**: 21 mph (34 kph)

Learning About the Creatures Around Us!

★<u>**Status**</u>: Least Concern

★<u>**Weight**</u>: 77–143 lbs. (35-64 kg)

★<u>**Where do they live?**</u>: They live in Central and South America by water (rivers and streams).

★The largest rodent in the world (other rodents-mice, squirrels, and porcupines).

★They are fantastic swimmers and love to be in the water. They will even sleep with their bodies under the water with only their nose above the water.

★They have partially webbed feet, which helps them be great swimmers.

★They can hold their breath for about 5 minutes underwater while diving to find plants to eat.

★They are most active at dusk.

★Some people have them as pets.

★Since they are very social animals, they will make friends with different species, and sometimes, these animals will sit or lay on the backs of capybaras.

Learning About the Creatures Around Us!

Fainting Goats (Tennessee Fainting Goat)

★**Animal class**: **Mammals** - (They are warm-blooded (the body temperature stays about the same temperature without help from the sun), breathe air with lungs, have a 4 chamber heart, have 3 bones in their inner ears, have vertebrae (a backbone or spine), have hair or fur (even whales and dolphins have some hair near their mouths), almost all species have a live birth, but 2 species lay eggs (the platypus and the echidna), all females produce (their bodies make) milk for their young, most have 4 legs or for humans, 2 arms and 2 legs, sizes range from the **Bumblebee bat** at 1 in (3 cm) to the **Blue whale** at 100 ft (30 m)) **(Examples: Whales, people, dogs, and elephants. There are about 6,500 different species.)**

★**Diet**: **Herbivore (They only eat plants)**- Grass, shrubs, leaves, bushes, and virtually any edible plant

★**Lifespan**: 10-18 years

★**Predators**: Coyotes, wolves, bobcats, and mountain lions

★**Size**: 17-25 in (43-64 cm) tall

★**Species**: There is only 1 species of this goat, but there are about 200 different species of goats

★**Status**: Endangered, about 10,000 left

Learning About the Creatures Around Us!

★<u>**Weight**</u>: 60-174 lbs. (27-79 kg)

★<u>**Where do they live?**</u>: They live throughout the world, except Antarctica.

★The first record of these goats came around the 1800s in Tennessee, U.S.A., when a farmer brought four goats with him when he moved to Tennessee. There is little information about the farmer and his origins, but some researchers think he might have been from Nova Scotia. Scientists are still trying to discover more about where these goats originated from.

★When something surprises or frightens them, their muscles go stiff for a short time, and they fall over or "faint." Their muscles freeze for up to 20 seconds, but it doesn't hurt them. Their fainting spell is a medical condition called Myotonia, which these goats are born with.

★They make great pets because they are not great jumpers and are very friendly. For many years in Tennessee, there has been a "Fainting Goat Festival" with food, live music, games for the whole family, and goat competitions.

Learning About the Creatures Around Us!

7 continents map with 5 oceans

Fireflies or Lightning Bugs

★**Animal class**: **Insects** (Have a segmented body (3 main body parts the head, the thorax, and the abdomen), cold-blooded, an exoskeleton (an outer skeleton around the whole body to help protect them), jointed legs, six legs, antennas, wings (some insect will have 1-2 pairs of wings or no wings at all), most babies come from eggs, but some are live births, and their sizes range from the **Dicopomorpha echmepterygis (a type of wasp, also called a Fairyfly)** at 0.005 in (.139 mm) to the **Phoebaeticus chani (a type of Stick insect)** at 2 ft (62.4 cm) long. **(Examples: Beetles, butterflies, Praying mantis, and ladybugs) There are around 925 thousand different species)**

★**Diet**: **Omnivore (They eat plants and meat)**- Dew droplets, pollen, or nectar from flowers, but some species do smaller insects

★**Lifespan**: About two months

★**Predators**: Birds, spiders, frogs, and lizards

★**Size**: 1 in (2.5 cm) long

★**Species**: There are about 2,000 different species

★**Status**: Threatened

★**Weight:** 0.0007 oz (20 mg)

Learning About the Creatures Around Us!

★<u>**Where do they live?**</u>: Live on every continent except Antarctica

★They live in warmer or tropical areas and are found in almost every habitat.

★They produce light from their tails, and it is called bioluminescent. Even some of the eggs and larvae of these species will have a slight glow.

★They make this light to help protect themselves from predators.

★They talk to each other with their lights and warn predators to stay away. This light also plays a huge role in finding a mate.

★They are poisonous to some animals when eaten but not poisonous to the touch.

Learning About the Creatures Around Us!

Firefly Squid

★**Animal class**: **Mollusks** (Invertebrates (with no backbone or spine) have an exoskeleton (an outer shell to help protect their soft bodies and have a sharp tongue called a "radula" that helps them take food off of hard surfaces, they breathe with tiny gills called ctenidia, they lay eggs, some have a "foot" (the underside of a snail) to help them move, and their sizes range from the **Acmella nana (a type of snail)** at 0.02 in (0.6 mm) to the **Colossal Squid** at 45 ft (14 m))**(Examples: Octopus, squid, snails, and clams. There are over 80,000 different species)**

★**Diet**: **Carnivore (They only eat meat)**- Crustaceans, small fishes, crabs, and shrimp

★**Lifespan**: About one year

★**Predators**: Whales, sharks, fish, squid, and crabs

★**Size**: 3 in (7.5 cm) tall

★**Species**: There is only one species of this kind, but there are about 300 different kinds of squid

★**Status**: Least Concern

★**Weight**: 0.31 oz (9 g)

★<u>**Where do they live?**</u>: Lives off the coast of Japan, the western Pacific Ocean.

★They have bioluminescence (makes their light), and this helps them talk to each other, confuse their predators to think they are bigger than they are, or attract prey. They can also camouflage into their surroundings.

★Some females will lay eggs fertilized by the male in the water, then the egg attaches to a hard surface, and some females will lay eggs and fertilize them themselves and attach them to a hard surface, then take their next form.

★Lights can be in unison or an alternate in a pattern.

★You can find them at a depth of 600-1200 ft (183-366 m) during the day, and they come to the surface to hunt and lay their eggs at night.

★They can be eaten by humans either cooked or raw (uncooked) and in the springtime.

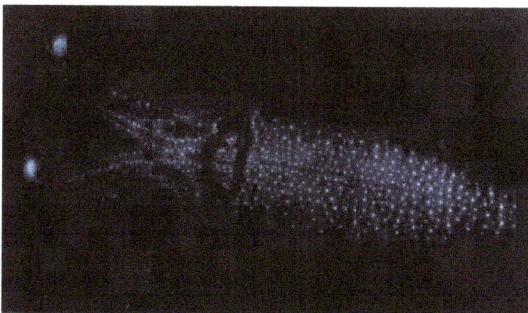

Gerenuk

★<u>**Animal class**</u>: **Mammals**-(They are warm-blooded (the body temperature stays about the same temperature without help from the sun), breathe air with lungs, have a 4 chamber heart, have 3 bones in their inner ears, have vertebrae (a backbone or spine), have hair or fur (even whales and dolphins have some hair near their mouths), almost all species have a live birth, but 2 species lay eggs (the platypus and the echidna), all females produce (their bodies make) milk for their young, most have 4 legs or for humans, 2 arms and 2 legs, sizes range from the <u>**Bumblebee bat**</u> at 1 in (3 cm) to the <u>**Blue whale**</u> at 100 ft (30 m)) **(Examples: Whales, people, dogs, and elephants. There are about 6,500 different species.)**

★<u>**Diet**</u>: **Herbivore (They only eat plants)**- Grass, herbs, leaves, flowers, and fruit

★<u>**Lifespan**</u>: 10 to 12 years

★<u>**Predators**</u>: Leopards, lions, jackals, and wild dogs

★<u>**Size**</u>: Between 3-3.5 ft (90-105 cm) tall & 4.6-5.3 ft (140-160 cm) long

★<u>**Species**</u>: There are only 1 species with long necks, but there are about 90 species of antelope

Learning About the Creatures Around Us!

★<u>**Speed:**</u> About 35 mph (56 kph)

★<u>**Status**</u>: Near Threatened

★<u>**Weight**</u>: 63 to 128 lbs. (29 to 58 kg)

★<u>**Where do they live?**</u>: They live in the Horn of Africa and the drier parts of East Africa.

★Only the males have horns.

★They like woodland forests, deserts, and open plains.

★The gerenuk eats standing on two legs to be able to reach leaves that are high up.

★They have to drink water like most other land animals. They get their water through the leaves that they eat.

Learning About the Creatures Around Us!

Glass Frogs

★<u>**Animal class**</u>: **Amphibians** (Have vertebrae (backbone or spine), are cold-blooded (their bodies cannot hold heat and must warm themselves by their surroundings like the sun), and can live on land and in the water, they lay their eggs in the water after the eggs hatch they go through metamorphosis (their bodies change) and start as a tadpole with gills, and will then change into their adult form and grow 4 legs and lungs, their skin does not have fur or feathers and helps them take in oxygen, and their sizes from the <u>**Paedophryne amauensis (a type of frog)**</u> at 0.27 in (0.7 mm) to the <u>**Chinese giant salamander**</u> at 6ft (2 m)) **(Examples: Frog, toads, salamanders, and newts. There are over 8,000 different species)**

★<u>**Diet**</u>: **Carnivore (They only eat meat)**- Insects, spiders, and worms

★<u>**Lifespan**</u>: About 14 years

★<u>**Predators**</u>: Snakes, birds, monkeys, and wasps

★<u>**Size**</u>: 0.78-3 in (about 2- 8 cm)

★<u>**Species**</u>: There are between 120-150 different species of glass frogs, but there are over 7,000 different species of frogs

★<u>**Status**</u>: Endangered

Learning About the Creatures Around Us!

★<u>**Weight**</u>: 1-3 oz (28-85 g)

★<u>**Where do they live?**</u>: They live in Central and South America.

★They live up in the mountains and lower lands in the rainforest trees and are always near water where they can lay their eggs.

★They are not poisonous.

★Some species are nocturnal (sleep during the day and awake at night) and will hunt at night

★One species has yellow spots on its back to look like the sunlight coming through the trees. These colors act like camouflage. During the night, these spots glow in the dark. ★Sometimes, their skin is see-through, and you can see their heart beating and internal organs.

★They can jump about 10 ft (3 m) in one jump.

Learning About the Creatures Around Us!

Green Basilisk Lizard (Jesus Christ Lizard)

★**Animal class**: **Reptiles-** (Their bodies are covered in bony plates or scales, they breathe air with lungs, are cold-blooded (their bodies cannot hold heat and must warm themselves by their surroundings like the sun), have vertebrae (spine or backbone), most have 4 legs, they lay eggs (Some species like the Viper (snake) will keep their eggs in their bodies until the egg hatches. Then the baby is born. A few rare species have a live birth like the Three-toed skink), and their sizes range from the **Brookesia nana (a chameleon)** at .55 in (1.4 cm) to the **Saltwater crocodile** at 20 ft (6 m)) **(Example: Lizards, turtles, snakes, and alligators. There are about 9,000 different species.)**

★**Diet**: **Omnivore (They eat plants and meat)-** Insects, fruit, plants, and small animals

★**Lifespan**: Up to 10 years

★**Predators**: Snakes and birds

★**Size**: 2-2.5 ft (60- 76 cm) (including the tail)

★**Species**: There are 4 different species of Basilisk lizards, but there are over 6,500 different species of lizards

Learning About the Creatures Around Us!

★**Speed**: 15 mph (24.1 kph) running on land & 7 mph (11 kph) running on water

★**Status**: Least Concern

★**Weight**: Up to 7 oz (198 g)

★**Where do they live?**: They live in Central and South America and can be found near rivers and streams in the rainforest.

★They spend a lot of their time up in trees, but when they sense danger, they can drop out of the tree and run away on the water.

★They are not poisonous.

★They have a unique ability to run on water because they have special toes on their rear feet.

★When they run on water, they pump their legs rapidly, slapping their feet hard against the water, and can run about 20 ft (6 m) before they sink into the water.

★These lizards are also fast swimmers and can hold their breath for up to 30 minutes.

Learning About the Creatures Around Us!

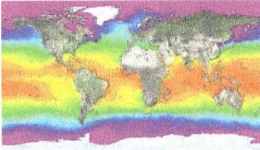

Hairy Frogfish

★<u>**Animal class**</u>: **Fish** (Have vertebrae (a backbone or spine), have gills instead of lungs, are cold-blooded (their bodies cannot hold heat and must warm themselves by their surroundings like the sun), have fins to help them get around, most have scales, most do not have eyelids, have a swim bladder (helps them control how deep they go in the water), they have a 2 chamber heart, their ears are inside their bodies, they lay eggs that will, but some females will carry their fertilized eggs and give live birth (only a few species do this), and their sizes range from a male **<u>Photocorynus spiniceps (a type of anglerfish)</u>** 0.2 in (6.1 mm) to the **<u>Whale shark</u>** at 42 ft (13 m)) **(Examples: Goldfish, sharks, salmon, and Sword Fish. There are over 30,000 different species)**

★<u>**Diet**</u>: **Carnivore (They only eat meat)**: Fish, snails, shrimp, crabs, and other small ocean animals, even other frogfish

★<u>**Lifespan**</u>: They can live up to 20 years

★<u>**Predators**</u>: Birds, eels, bigger fish, and other frogfish

★<u>**Size**</u>: Anywhere from 2-15 in (about 5.08-38 cm)

★<u>**Species**</u>: There are about 46 known species of frogfish, but there are around 30,000 different species of fish

★<u>**Status:**</u> Not threatened

Learning About the Creatures Around Us!

★<u>**Weight**</u>: About 1.16 oz (.033 kg)

★<u>**Where do they live?**</u>: They are found nearly worldwide in tropical and temperate seas.

★Many can change color over time to camouflage within their surroundings (sometimes days or weeks).

★Their attack is amongst the fastest in the world.

★They have a unique lure (antennae) and wave it in front of their head (just like how we traditionally fish with lines and lures) to attract small fish and shrimp to come closer.

★Most often, they move by jumping and walking along the seafloor. To "jump," the frogfish will suck in water through its mouth and force it out through its gills. This action makes them jet-propelled (pushes them forward with water)!

Learning About the Creatures Around Us!

Ibex

★**Animal class**: **Mammals -** (They are warm-blooded (the body temperature stays about the same temperature without help from the sun), breathe air with lungs, have a 4 chamber heart, have 3 bones in their inner ears, have vertebrae (a backbone or spine), have hair or fur (even whales and dolphins have some hair near their mouths), almost all species have a live birth, but 2 species lay eggs (the platypus and the echidna), all females produce (their bodies make) milk for their young, most have 4 legs or for humans, 2 arms and 2 legs, sizes range from the **Bumblebee bat** at 1 in (3 cm) to the **Blue whale** at 100 ft (30 m)) **(Examples: Whales, people, dogs, and elephants. There are about 6,500 different species.)**

★**Diet**: **Herbivores (They only eat plants)**-Grass, herbs, and plant leaves

★**Lifespan**: About 17 years

★**Predators**: Leopards, eagles, and large birds

★**Size**: 2-3 ft (60-90 cm)

★**Species**: There are 5 different species of ibex

★**Speed:** About 45 mph (72 kph)

Where learning language online is fun!

Learning About the Creatures Around Us!

★<u>**Status**</u>: Least Concern

★<u>**Weight**</u>: About 65-265 lbs. (30-120 kg)

★<u>**Where do they live?**</u>: They live in Europe, north-central Asia, and northern Africa

★They are a kind of wild mountain goat that lives on the sides of mountains and rocky hills but can also be found in grasslands and forests. They live in mountain ranges like the Alps and the Himalayas at high elevations.

★They can jump more than 6 ft (1.8 m) straight up.

★Their hooves act like suction cups, which helps them run fast on rocky cliff sides.

★Both females and males have horns, but the males are larger and more curved. They use them to help fight off Predators and to compete for a mate.

★The Ibex lives in a herd of about 15-20, with one male in charge.

★Male ibex also have beards.

★A small bird called a Grackle will pick and eat the bugs off the Ibex. The Ibex gives the birds food, and it stays clean. This kind of friendship is called a symbiotic relationship (each animal helps the other, and many animals have relationships like this).

Learning LOL

Where learning language online is fun!

Learning About the Creatures Around Us!

Immortal Jellyfish

★**Animal class**: **Scyphozoa** (They are called "true jellyfish," they have a bell or an umbrella shape, have tentacles (long thin string-like arms to help them eat, move around, and protect themselves), have soft jelly-like bodies with no bones or vertebrae, have no brain, eyes, heart, have no digestive tract (this means that their food go in and out of the same hole) the females will lay eggs that the male in the water fertilizes then the egg attaches to a hard surface, and then the lifecycle begins, and their sizes rang from the **Irukandji box jellyfish** at .8 in (2 mm) to the **Lion Mane jellyfish** at 120 ft (37 m))**(Examples: Fried Egg jellyfish, Immortal jellyfish, Bloodybelly Comb jellyfish, and Box jellyfish) There are around 2,000 different species)**

★**Diet**: **Carnivore (They only eat meat)**-Plankton, fish eggs, and small mollusks

★**Lifespan**: When it is physically damaged or even starved, they go back to a polyp (or a baby) and starts the growth process over again, so they could live forever if not eaten

★**Predators**: Bigger jellyfish, sea anemones, fish, sharks, sea turtles, and penguins

★**Size**: About 0.18 in (4.5 mm) big

© 2023   Learninglol.com   37

Learning About the Creatures Around Us!

★**Species**: There is only 1 in its species, but there are over 2,000 different species of jellyfish

★**Status**: Not Threatened

★**Weight**: About .03 oz. (1 g)

★**Where do they live?**: They are found in warm ocean waters around the world, like the Pacific, Indian, and Atlantic Oceans.

★They are mainly transparent (clear) with a bright red stomach and are bell-shaped with about 90 tentacles.

★Jellyfish do not have brains but have nerves in their tentacles to help them touch the things around them, sense water temperature, and help catch prey.

★They can sting you, but they will not kill you. It will just hurt.

★They have amazing regenerating (to regrow) abilities. They can regrow their tentacles and turn themselves back into babies to heal their whole body.

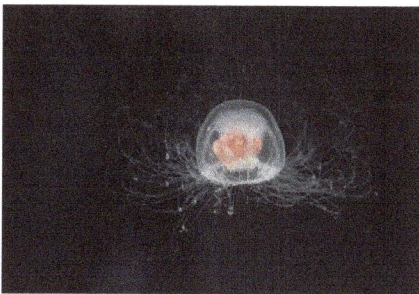

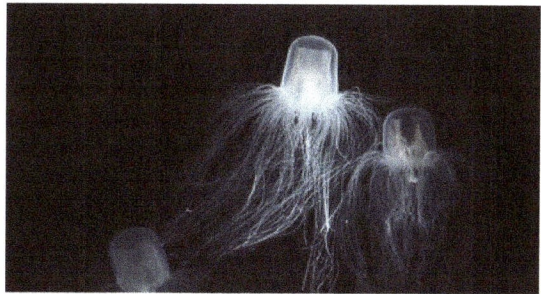

Learning About the Creatures Around Us!

Japanese Spider Crab

★**Animal class:** **Crustaceans**- (Have a segmented body with 3 main body parts (the head, the thorax, and the abdomen) and an exoskeleton (an outer skeleton around the whole body to help protect them) when it is time to grow they will "molt" (get rid of their old exoskeleton), they breathe with gills (land crabs have lungs and gills so that they can switch when they are on land or in the water), 2 pairs of antennae and 10 legs, they lay eggs that are sometimes attached to a long string or other objects in the water or in a pouch attached to the animal, and their sizes range from the **Stygotantulus Stocki** (similar to shrimp) at 0.004 in (0.1 mm) to the **Japanese spider crab** at 7 ft (2 m)) **(Examples: Crabs, shrimp, lobsters, and pill bugs. There are about 40,000 different species.)**

★**Diet**: **Omnivores (They eat plants and meat)**: Shrimp, seaweed, fish, lobsters, and they will also eat dead plants and animals that they find on the ocean floor

★**Lifespan:** They can live up to 100 years

★**Predators:** Octopus and humans

★**Size:** About 3-7 ft (1-2 m), and their 10 legs alone are about 2.5 ft (76 cm) long

★**Species:** There are about 5,000 different kinds of crabs in the world

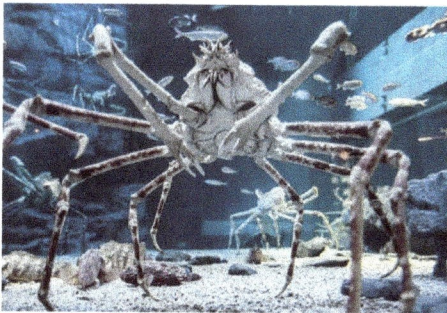

Learning About the Creatures Around Us!

★**Status:** Not Threatened

★**Weight:** About 40 lbs. (18 kg)

★**Where do they live?:** They live in the Pacific Ocean near Japan and sometimes can be seen in the waters near China and Taiwan, but it is rare.

★They can go as deep as 160-2500 ft (50-762 m).

★They have a hard and bumpy outer shell (exoskeleton) that is orange-tan with white spots, and they sometimes use seaweed to cover their bodies. Their bumpy shells and the seaweed help them camouflage from predators.

★People eat these crabs, which are considered a delicacy (fancy food). But you cannot fish for these crabs during their mating season, from January to April.

★During mating season, these crabs will go to shallower waters to lay their eggs. Females will lay about 1 million eggs, but only a few will reach adulthood.

★They can lose up to 3 limbs and still get around, and sometimes, when they molt (get a new skin), they can regenerate (regrow) a new limb.

★Spider crabs can molt about 20 times during their lifetime.

Learning About the Creatures Around Us!

Jerboa

★<u>**Animal class**</u>: **Mammals** - (They are warm-blooded (the body temperature stays about the same temperature without help from the sun), breathe air with lungs, have a 4 chamber heart, have 3 bones in their inner ears, have vertebrae (a backbone or spine), have hair or fur (even whales and dolphins have some hair near their mouths), almost all species have a live birth, but 2 species lay eggs (the platypus and the echidna), all females produce (their bodies make) milk for their young, most have 4 legs or for humans, 2 arms and 2 legs, sizes range from the <u>**Bumblebee bat**</u> at 1 in (3 cm) to the <u>**Blue whale**</u> at 100 ft (30 m)) **(Examples: Whales, people, dogs, and elephants. There are about 6,500 different species.)**

★<u>**Diet**</u>: **Omnivore (They eat plants and meat)**- Plants and small insects

★<u>**Lifespan**</u>: About 6 years

★<u>**Predators**</u>: Owls, foxes, cats, jackals, and snakes

★<u>**Size**</u>: 2-6 in (5-15 cm) in length & long tails of 2.5-9 in (7-25 cm)

★<u>**Species**</u>: There are 33 different jerboa species

★<u>**Speed**</u>: 15 mph (24 kph)

Learning About the Creatures Around Us!

★<u>Status</u>: Some species are Near Threatened, some are Least Concern, and some are Vulnerable

★<u>Weight</u>: About 0.8-1.3 oz (22 g)

★<u>Where do they live?</u>: They can be found in Asia and Northern Africa, in the grasslands and deserts

★They are a kind of rodent (like mice and hamsters

★They can jump between 6-9 ft (2-3 m) into the air in 1 jump.

★Jerboas have an excellent sense of smell and great hearing.

★They like to live underground in a burrow but will find higher ground to make their homes during the rainy season.

★They are nocturnal (they sleep during the day and hunt at night), which is helpful because temperatures can be extremely hot in some of their habitats. In deserts, temperatures can reach 130 F (55 C).

★Jerboas also have a special flap of skin on their ears to help prevent (stop) sand from entering them.

Learning About the Creatures Around Us!

Leaf Tail Gecko

★**Animal class**: **Reptiles-**(Their bodies are covered in bony plates or scales, they breathe air with lungs, are cold-blooded (their bodies cannot hold heat and must warm themselves by their surroundings like the sun), have vertebrae (spine or backbone), most have 4 legs, they lay eggs (Some species like the Viper (snake) will keep their eggs in their bodies until the egg hatches. Then the baby is born. A few rare species have a live birth like the Three-toed skink), and their sizes range from the **Brookesia nana (a chameleon)** at .55 in (1.4 cm) to the **Saltwater crocodile** at 20 ft (6 m)) **(Example: Lizards, turtles, snakes, and alligators. There are about 9,000 different species.)**

★**Diet**: **Carnivore (They only eat meat)**: Worms, spiders, small rodents, and bugs

★**Lifespan**: About 2-9 years

★**Predators**: Snakes, owls, eagles, and rats

★**Size**: About 4-12 in (10-30 cm)

★**Species**: There are about ten different species of Leaf tail geckos, but there are around 1,500 different species of geckos

★**Speed**: About 30 mph (48 kph)

Learning About the Creatures Around Us!

★<u>**Status**</u>: Near Threatened

★<u>**Weight**</u>: 0.35-1 oz (10 g-30 g)

★<u>**Where do they live?**</u>: The gecko lives in Madagascar and some smaller surroundings islands

★Since their tails look like leaves, they can camouflage into trees, bushes, and plants.

★These geckos do not have eyelids, so they use their tongues to keep their eyes wet and clean.

★If they lose their tails, they will regenerate (regrow) a new one. And if a gecko is trying to scare away a predator, it can actually "drop" its tail and try to escape.

★They have extraordinary feet that let them climb vertically up smooth surfaces like glass.

★They are nocturnal but lie in the warm sun during the day.

Learning About the Creatures Around Us!

Leatherback Turtle

★**Animal class**: **Reptiles**-(Their bodies are covered in bony plates or scales, they breathe air with lungs, are cold-blooded (their bodies cannot hold heat and must warm themselves by their surroundings like the sun), have vertebrae (spine or backbone), most have four legs, they lay eggs (Some species like the Viper (snake) will keep their eggs in their bodies until the egg hatches. Then the baby is born. A few rare species have a live birth like the Three-toed skink), and their sizes range from the **Brookesia nana (a chameleon)** at .55 in (1.4 cm) to the **Saltwater crocodile** at 20 ft (6 m)) **(Example: Lizards, turtles, snakes, and alligators. There are about 9,000 different species.)**

★**Diet**: **Omnivore (They eat plants and meat)**- Jellyfish, seaweed, and sea squirts

★**Lifespan**: They live around 30-40 years

★**Predators**: Plastic bags in the ocean (they get confused for jellyfish, not an animal, but still kill many turtles), sharks, and other large animals. Crabs, birds, cats, and dogs eat their eggs

★**Size**: about 4.5- 6.5 ft (1.5-2 m), but some are much bigger

★**Species**: Out of the seven different species of sea turtles, the leatherback is the largest. There are around 550 different species of turtles.

Learning About the Creatures Around Us!

★<u>**Speed**</u>: About 22 mph (35 kph)

★<u>**Status**</u>: Vulnerable

★<u>**Weight**</u>: 562-2,000 lbs. (255-900kg)

★<u>**Where do they live?**</u>: These turtles live in warm and tropical waters and sometimes be spotted in colder waters near Alaska.

★Their cartilage-like shells are covered with their rubbery skin, unlike other turtles, whose bony shells are on the outside, and we can see them.

★Their throats are covered with backward-facing spines. The spines help when they are eating jellyfish. Since Leatherback turtles do not have teeth (their mouth is more like a beck), so the jellyfish cannot escape.

★Females go to warm tropical beaches to make their nests for their eggs, but they usually never choose the same beach each year. Here, the nests are vulnerable to Predators.

★They can dive about 4,000 ft (1,200 m), and if needed, they can hold their breath for about 75 minutes, depending on their actions.

★They also travel thousands of miles (km) a year between where they nest and eat.

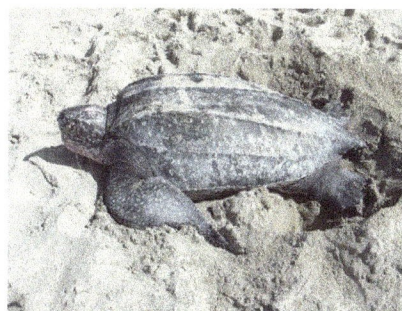

Learning About the Creatures Around Us!

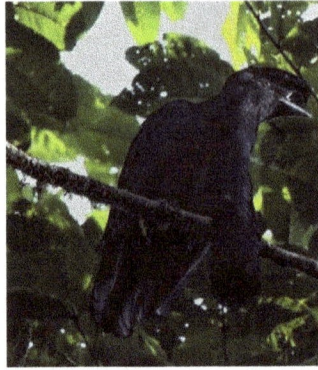

Long-wattled Umbrellabird

★**Animal class**: **Birds** (Have feathers, a beak (no teeth), two legs, two wings (some species cannot fly), have vertebrae (spine or backbone), are warm-blooded (the body temperature stays about the same temperature), lay eggs, might be related to dinosaurs, have a four-chamber heart (4 parts), most have great eyesight, and they range in size from the **Bee hummingbird** at 2.2 in (5.5 cm) to the **Ostrich** at 9 ft (3 m) tall) **(Examples: Penguins, parrots, owls, and hawks) There are around 11,000 different species)**

★**Diet**: **Omnivore (They eat plants and meat)**- Insects, frogs, and fruits

★**Lifespan**: Up to 20 years

★**Predators**: Monkeys, snakes, and some larger birds

★**Size**: 11 in (28 cm) long

★**Species**: There are three known species, but there are 11,000 different species of birds

★**Status**: Endangered- an estimated 15,000 remaining because of habitat destruction and climate change

Learning About the Creatures Around Us!

★<u>**Weight**</u>: Up to 1 lbs. (.45 kg)

★<u>**Where do they live?**</u>: They live in Ecuador and Colombia

★They do not fly well, will fly for a short distance, and will walk around in the canopy of the trees.

★On the tops of their heads, they have feathers in the shape of an umbrella. These feathers are where they get their names.

★The males carry a long wattle from their chin, about 14 in (35 cm) long and covered in short, scaly feathers. It is for courtship displays. When he sees a mate, he will puff up his wattle, which looks like a pinecone, and make a special low-sounding call. Scientists think these feathers might help their sound go farther.

★Some females will have a wattle, but it will be much smaller than males.

Learning About the Creatures Around Us!

Mongoose

★**Animal class**: **Mammals -** (They are warm-blooded (the body temperature stays about the same temperature without help from the sun), breathe air with lungs, have a 4 chamber heart, have 3 bones in their inner ears, have vertebrae (a backbone or spine), have hair or fur (even whales and dolphins have some hair near their mouths), almost all species have a live birth, but 2 species lay eggs (the platypus and the echidna), all females produce (their bodies make) milk for their young, most have 4 legs or for humans, 2 arms and 2 legs, sizes range from the **Bumblebee bat** at 1 in (3 cm) to the **Blue whale** at 100 ft (30 m)) **(Examples: Whales, people, dogs, and elephants. There are about 6,500 different species.)**

★**Diet**: **Omnivores (They eat plants and meat)**: Nuts, berries, frogs, black mambas and other types of snakes, seeds, eggs, worms, and some birds

★**Lifespan**: About 9 years in the wild and about 20 in captivity

★**Predators**: Black mambas and other types of snakes, large birds, leopards, jackals, and storks

★**Speed**: About 20 mph (32 kph)

★**Size**: 7 in-2 ft (18-60 cm)

★**Species**: There are about 34 different species

Learning About the Creatures Around Us!

★<u>**Status**</u>: Threatened (most of the 34 species)

★<u>**Weight**</u>: 1-12 lbs. (0.5-5 kg)

★<u>**Where do they live?**</u>: They live in Africa and some parts of Asia

★They live in many different environments. Some live in deserts, grasslands, close to rivers, and Tropical forests. They like to burrow and make tunnels for themselves, and some like to be in trees.

★They can fight a venomous snake like the Black Mamba or a Cobra and win. Mongooses are immune to their venom, which will not affect them when bitten.

★They can also swim and dive underwater to look for food.

★Mongooses have been used to help with pest control (snakes and mice) on some tropical islands (not their native habitat) like Hawaii. Unfortunately, this did not work in many cases, and they killed many of the native species and caused more trouble than the snakes and mice. Many countries banned them for this reason.

Learning About the Creatures Around Us!

Sea Bunny Slug

★**Animal class**: **Mollusks** (Are invertebrates (with no backbone or spine), have an exoskeleton (an outer shell to help protect their soft bodies and have a sharp tongue called a "radula" that helps them take food off of hard surfaces, they breathe with tiny gills called ctenidia, they lay eggs, some have a "foot" (the underside of a snail) to help them move, and their sizes range from the **Acmella nana (a type of snail)** at 0.02 in (0.6 mm) to the **Colossal Squid** at 45 ft (14 m))**(Examples: Octopus, squid, snails, and clams. There are over 80,000 different species)**

★**Diet**: **Omnivores (They eat plants and meat)**: Algae, sponges, seagrass, and snails

★**Lifespan**: A few months to 1 year

★**Predators**: Birds and turtles

★**Size**: About 1 in (3 cm)

★**Species**: There are about 16 different species of Sea slugs, but only one that looks like a rabbit

★**Status**: Not Known

★**Weight**: Unknown

Learning About the Creatures Around Us!

★<u>**Where do they live?**</u>: They live in the Indian Ocean, near Japan, Africa, the Philippines, and Australia.

★You can find them on the ocean floor on rocks and coral, and sometimes you can even see them swimming near the ocean's surface.

★They are covered in needle-like tub structures (sensory organs) that look like fur, their "ears" are sensory organs like antennas, and their gills are on their backside and look like a tail.

★They have very poor eyesight and can only see dark and light.

★They are very poisonous and eat animals like poisonous sponges to help themselves become more poisonous.

★ Scientists are studying sea bunnies because their toxin might be able to help with cancer drugs and treatments.

Learning About the Creatures Around Us!

7 continents map with 5 oceans

Sea Squirts

★**Animal class**: **Ascidiacea** (Are invertebrates (with no backbone or exoskeleton (an outer skeleton around the whole body to help protect them)), have a rough and sometimes thick or thin outer skin called a "tunic" (made from cellulose and acts like an exoskeleton), have 2 openings for water and food entering and exiting the body, the do not need a mate to reproduce (to have a baby), after the egg fertilizes, a tadpole like Ascidiacea swims using its tail to find a hard surface, once attached it will go through a metamorphosis (their bodies change) where they will absorb (eat) their brain, eye, and spine for nutrients since they will live there forever and will change into their final form, and their sizes range from the **Minipera pedunculata (a type of sea squirt)** at 0.02 in (0.05 mm) to the **Antarctic Distaplia cylindrica (an attached colony of sea squirts)** at 23 ft (7 m)) **(Examples: Skeleton Panda sea squirt, Sea pineapple sea squirt, Star tunicate, and Sea Potato sea squirt) There are around 2,000 different species)**

★**Diet**: **Omnivores (They eat plants and meat)**: Algae, plankton, bacteria, and the remains of dead plants and animals

★**Lifespan**: 7-30 years

★**Predators**: Eels, fish, starfish, sharks, and snails

★**Size**: 0.3-5 in (0.7-12 cm)

★**Species**: There are 2,000 different species

Where learning language online is fun!

Learning About the Creatures Around Us!

★**Speed**: These animals can move 0.7 in (2 cm) a day

★**Status**: Not Endangered

★**Weight**: About 4-7 oz (0.1-0.2 kg)

★**Where do they live?**: They live in every ocean, from the cold Arctic to the warm tropical Indian Ocean.

★They can be found in the deep and shallow parts of the ocean. And they will attach themselves to rocks, seashells, docks, and boats moving across the world.

★Most of these species are poisonous.

★When they are born, they have a brain, but once finding a place to call home, they will absorb (eat) their brain. Since they will stay in the same place for their whole lives, they do not need a brain. When they absorb (eat) their brains, this gives them nutrients (food) until their next meal floats in front of them.

★ People can find this animal in many shapes and sizes. They can be almost every color and have shapes like tubes, hearts, bells, plant-like, and even a skeleton (the panda sea squirt).

★When you take this animal out of the water, it will squirt the water out of its body. The squirting water is where the Sea squirt gets its name.

★Some species can be eaten by people and enjoyed by many countries.

Learning About the Creatures Around Us!

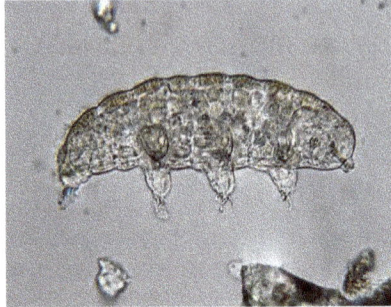

Tardigrades (Water Bear)

★**Animal class**: **Tardigrades** (Are invertebrates (with no backbone or exoskeleton (an outer skeleton around the whole body to help protect them), have fused (all together) 4 segmented bodies, have eight unjointed legs with 4-8 sharp claws on each leg, to reproduce (to have a baby) the males fertilize the eggs, and the female either carries the eggs or keeps them close, can withstand extremely cold, dry, or hot weather by going into a "tun" state (they dry their bodies out and turn onto a ball, and can live like this for many years), and their sizes range from the **Hypsibius Dujardini (a type of Water bear)** at 0.002 in (0.50 mm) to the **Echiniscoides Sigismondi (a type of water bear)** at 0.05 in (1.5 mm)) **(Examples: Water bears) There are around 1,000 different species)**

★**Diet**: **Omnivore (They eat plants and meat)**: Bacteria, the fluid of a plant, and animal cells, nematodes (roundworms), and other tardigrades

★**Lifespan**: Some species will live for only a few months, and others a few years. If they go into a dehydrated state, it could be much longer.

★**Predators**: Tardigrades, nematodes (roundworms), spiders, insect larvae (babies), and amoebas

★**Size**: 0.002 to 0.04 in (0.05 to 1.02 millimeters)

★**Species**: There are about 1,100 different species

Learning About the Creatures Around Us!

★**Status**: Not Threatened

★**Weight**: No known weight

★**Where do they live?**: They can survive almost anywhere there is water, the deep oceans, lakes, ponds, tall snow-covered mountains, and even space! (scientist did experiment).

★They can also survive solar ultraviolet radiation, temperatures colder than -328 F (-200 C) and hotter than 300 F (148.9 C), extreme pressure (like at the bottom of the ocean), being shot from a gun, and the vacuum of space.

★To withstand these extreme environments, these micro-animals squeeze all the water out of their bodies, tuck their heads and limbs into their bodies, and roll into a ball called a "tun." When their environments get better, they will return to their normal state. They can stay in a dehydrated, death-like state for five or more years. The oldest revived from this was 30 years.

★They do not have bones, but they have a hydroskeleton. Their hydroskeleton is where fluid-filled cavities, like jellyfish or earthworms, support the body.

★They are translucent (clear or see-through), but you can see them in the right light without a microscope.

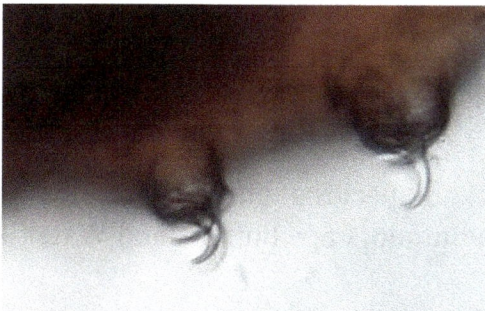

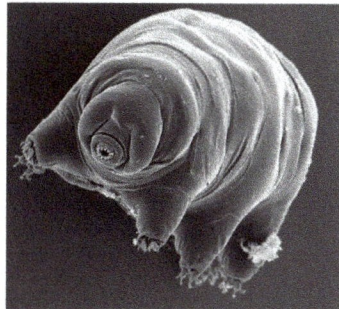

Learning About the Creatures Around Us!

Water Buffalo

★<u>**Animal class**</u>: **Mammals -** (They are warm-blooded (the body temperature stays about the same temperature without help from the sun), breathe air with lungs, have a 4 chamber heart, have 3 bones in their inner ears, have vertebrae (a backbone or spine), have hair or fur (even whales and dolphins have some hair near their mouths), almost all species have a live birth, but 2 species lay eggs (the platypus and the echidna), all females produce (their bodies make) milk for their young, most have 4 legs or for humans, 2 arms and 2 legs, sizes range from the <u>**Bumblebee bat**</u> at 1 in (3 cm) to the <u>**Blue whale**</u> at 100 ft (30 m)) **(Examples: Whales, people, dogs, and elephants. There are about 6,500 different species.)**

★<u>**Diet**</u>: **Herbivores (They only eat plants)**: Grass, plants, fruit, tree bark, herbs, and bushes

★<u>**Lifespan**</u>: About 25 years

★<u>**Predators**</u>: Tigers, humans, crocodiles, and leopards

★<u>**Size**</u>: About 6 ft (183 cm) tall, and their horns are about 5ft (152 cm) wide

★<u>**Species**</u>: There are about 74 different sub-species of buffalo, but only three species of water buffalo: American buffalo, Cape buffalo, and Water buffalo.

Learning About the Creatures Around Us!

★<u>**Speed**</u>: About 30 mph (49 kph)

★<u>**Status**</u>: Endangered (about 4,000 wild buffalo left)

★<u>**Weight**</u>: 1,400-2,600 lbs. (635-1,180 kg)

★<u>**Where do they live?**</u>: The wild water buffalo live in the tropical regions of China and Southeast Asia but are on every continent. (You will not find them in the Arctic or Antarctic).

★People have been using these animals for about 5,000 years. They would use them for their meat, milk, horns, and fur to help travelers on their farmlands and carry heavy loads. People today still use the water buffalo in the same way.

★People have used their horns for medicine, jewelry, musical instruments, and more.

★They are excellent swimmers! They will spend most of their days in the muddy swamp water to cool off (they don't have sweat glands to stay cool) and even dive under the water to find plants to eat.

Learning About the Creatures Around Us!

Wobbegong Shark

★**Animal class**: **Fish** (Have vertebrae (a backbone or spine), have gills instead of lungs, are cold-blooded (their bodies cannot hold heat and must warm themselves by their surroundings like the sun), have fins to help them get around, most have scales, most do not have eyelids, have a swim bladder (helps them control how deep they go in the water), they have a 2-chamber heart, their ears are inside their bodies, lay eggs that will, but some females will carry their fertilized eggs and give live birth (only a few species do this), and their sizes range from a male **Photocorynus spiniceps (a type of anglerfish)** 0.2 in (6.1 mm) to the **Whale shark** at 42 ft (13 m)) **(Examples: Goldfish, sharks, salmon, and Sword Fish. There are over 30,000 different species)**

★**Diet**: **Carnivore (They only eat meat)**- Octopus, fish, smaller sharks, lobsters, and crab

★**Lifespan**: Unknown, but Marine biologists estimate around 20-30 years (more research is currently underway)

★**Predators**: Larger sharks, larger fish, and orcas

★**Size**: about 3- 6 ft (1-2 m)

★**Species**: There are about 12 species of Wobbegong sharks, but there are around 500 species of sharks

★**Status**: Least Concern

Learning About the Creatures Around Us!

★<u>**Weight**</u>: About 154 lbs. (70 kg)

★<u>**Where do they live?**</u>: These sharks swim in the western Pacific Ocean near Australia and Japan

★They are nocturnal (awake at night and sleeping during the day) and hunt at night.

★Sometimes called a "Carpet shark" because they can camouflage well on the bottom of the ocean floor, especially around reefs.

★Other sharks need to move to breathe, but the Wobbegong shark does not need to keep moving to breathe.

★They can be found in tide pools at low tide, and when the tide comes back in, they will swim back to sea.

★This shark will lay on the ocean floor and wait for prey to swim by. It will inhale the prey and then swallow it whole. They will even eat animals significantly larger than themselves. It will hold the animal in its mouth until it dies and then chews it.

Learning LOL

Where learning language online is fun!

Don't forget to check out our other books, Daily Vocabulary Worksheets Volume 1 and 2 & Daily Vocabulary Flashcards Volume 1 and 2.

www.ingramcontent.com/pod-product-compliance
Lightning Source LLC
Chambersburg PA
CBHW080527030426
42337CB00023B/4658